Dogs

GROOVY TUBE BOOK™

FACT BOOK • ANIMALS • GAME BOARD

Written by Susan Ring
For Luka, Chloe, and, of course, Darla

Illustrated by Derek Bacon
To Vic: who honked instead of barked

Game by innovativeKids®
Special thanks to Martin Deeley, President of the International Association of Canine Professionals, and his wife, Pat Trichter-Deeley, for fact checking this book.

PHOTO CREDITS
P. 3: © Design Pics Inc./Alamy; p. 8 right: © Digital Vision/Getty Images; p. 10, 23: © Alley Cat Productions/Brand X Pictures/Getty Images; p. 11: © Medioimages/Alamy; p. 14: © PhotoStockFile/Alamy; p. 15 top: © Collette Parker/Alamy; p. 15 bottom: © Stan Fellerman/Alamy; p. 19 bottom, 23: © imagebroker/Alamy; p. 20, 23: © Alaska Stock LLC/Alamy; p. 21 left, 23: © Digital Archive Japan/Alamy

Man's Best Friend

It's hard to imagine a world without dogs. They run with us, they play with us, and they protect our homes and our families. Some dogs guide our way, some help us work, and others become celebrated heroes.

Dogs have been close companions to humans for thousands of years. Today, the major dog organizations have divided dogs into several main groups: working, herding, sporting, non-sporting, hounds, terriers, and toy breeds. But there are many combinations of breeds, too, and these are called mixed breeds.

Get ready to find out what all dogs have in common—and what makes each one so unique!

Mixed Breed

Vizsla

West Highland
White Terrier

Pekingese

Brittany

German
Shorthaired
Pointer

Basset
Hound

Doggone Relatives

From the start of recorded history, humans and dogs have been companions. Ancient cave paintings in France show humans and dogs hunting together. These paintings are over 14,000 years old. However, scientists believe that dogs originated as many as 60,000 years ago or more!

Coyotes, which look like small wolves, are close relatives of dogs. Coyotes can live just about anywhere, from hot deserts to chilly forests to steep mountains. In fact, many of them live in Beverly Hills and Hollywood!

In 1997, scientists tested the DNA of wolves, jackals, and coyotes to see which of these animals were our dogs' closest relatives. The test showed that the wolf is the true ancestor of present-day dogs.

Like dogs, wolves are social animals. They live in groups called packs. A wolf pack has a mother, father, aunts, uncles, and puppies. All of the adult wolves help raise the wolf pups. The wolf pack works together to hunt for food, be it something as big as a moose or as small as a mouse!

Coyote

Dingo

Wolf

Wild dogs called dingoes live in Australia. Scientists believe that they evolved from the pet dogs of Asian seafarers, which were brought to Australia around 5,000 years ago. Those dogs escaped into the wild and evolved into the dingoes of today.

Puppy Love

Nothing is more loveable than a soft, warm, cuddly puppy! When puppies are first born, they can't see or hear. After about 10 days, their eyes and ears begin to open. Soon they are playing around and, of course, getting into puppy trouble.

When a puppy is about a month old, it is finally strong enough to sit and stand on its own. At about 8 to 10 weeks old, it's ready to leave mom and say hello to a new home.

Golden Retriever Puppies

How old are you in dog years? People used to think that every human year was equal to 7 dog years. But puppies become adult dogs in just 2 years. So this is a better formula to use: Figure $10\frac{1}{2}$ dog years for each human year—but just for the first 2 years. After that, every human year equals 4 dog years. So if you're 8 years old, you'd be 45 in dog years!

Most mother dogs have between four and six puppies in a litter. As soon as the puppies are born, their mom licks them clean. Then they snuggle up to her belly and drink her milk.

As puppies grow, their baby teeth fall out and their new adult teeth come in. But as this happens, puppies need to teethe. And boy, do they! From shoes to TV remotes to hairbrushes—puppies like to chew!

Puppies also like to sleep a lot. They need to sleep to help their bodies grow. Dogs grow a lot in the first few months. They are almost their full size when they are 1 year old. They are not really considered to be adults until they are about 18 months old though.

Senses

you wish you could smell like a dog? —really *smell* like a dog? Dogs have super sense of smell and use it a great deal to get around in the world.

Some dogs can pick up a scent even if it's half a mile away. They can smell things under piles of leaves, deep snow, and even underwater.

Detectives often use bloodhounds and beagles to pick up the scent of missing people. Their sharp sense of smell can detect a person's scent weeks after that person has even been in the area.

Parson
Russell
Terriers

Why do dogs
just don't hear
hearing. Their
greater than that of

Not only can dogs hear better, their ears can change direction—like a satellite dish—picking up sounds from different angles. They can figure out where a sound is coming from in 6/100ths of a second!

Some dogs, such as
borzois, and whippets, are called sight hounds. They have excellent vision and will use their eyes rather than their noses to hunt.

Human noses have about 5 million cells that help us detect different smells. Dog noses can have as many as 225 million of these cells!

Dog Talk

Dogs might not be able to speak in words, but they sure have a lot to say. Dogs communicate with people and with other dogs in many different ways. To understand them, all you have to do is learn what their body language and sounds mean.

A bow can mean "won't you please play with me?" Rolling over may mean that the dog is letting you or another dog be the big boss.

The tail can tell you a lot! A wagging tail usually means the dog is happy—but this isn't true all the time. Sometimes a dog wags its tail when it is excited or agitated but not necessarily happy. When a dog puts its tail in between its legs, it is showing you that it's afraid and cautious.

Golden Retriever

Gr-r-r! A growl is a great warning sign that the dog is angry. If you don't pay attention and back away, a bite might be coming. When it wants to look even more ferocious, a dog pulls its upper lip back and exposes its sharp teeth.

One of the most ancient breeds of dog is the basenji. What's unique about this breed? It is the only breed that doesn't bark! The basenji's larynx, or voice box, is not in the same place in the throat as other breeds. It does growl, whine, and make a vocal sound when it's happy. Some say it sounds a bit like a yodel.

Dogs whine or bark loudly when they are upset. Just like wolves, some dogs howl when they miss their owners or other members of their pack.

Even a dog's fur can tell you something. Often, when a dog is angry, its hackles—hairs on the back of its neck and back—go up. When the dog no longer feels threatened, the hair lays back down.

Basenji

Big and Small

Dogs come in so many different shapes and sizes that sometimes it's hard to believe that they are all the same species.

The tallest of all breeds is the Irish wolfhound. These dogs stand about three feet tall at the shoulder! As their name says, they were originally bred to hunt wolves. During the 1800s, only royalty were allowed to keep Irish wolfhounds. As a result, the breed almost disappeared altogether.

Another giant breed, the Great Dane, is known for its sweet personality. Sometimes people call this type of dog a gentle giant.

Great Dane

Great Danes can weigh as much as 200 pounds! Even a Great Dane puppy less than a year old can weigh 120 pounds.

The smallest breed of dog is the Chihuahua. These little dogs can weigh as little as three pounds. Some are so tiny that they can fit inside a teacup! In spite of their size, they are brave little creatures and often behave as if they were giants.

Some dogs, like dachshunds and basset hounds, are longer than they are tall! Dachshunds were bred to dig badgers out from their dens in the ground. And the basset hound, with its long body and droopy ears, can weigh as much as 70 pounds!

Dachshund

The chunkiest canine on record was a dog named Zorba. He was an Old English mastiff, which is a giant breed to begin with. A hefty weight for a male mastiff is about 200 pounds. Zorba weighed in at more than 340 pounds!

Furry or Not

What is one thing that makes dogs look so very different from each other? Their fur! Some dogs have so much fur that you can't even see their faces. The Old English sheepdog was bred to herd sheep in the cold, damp weather of the British Isles. Its thick outer coat keeps it warm, and its undercoat is waterproof.

Another sheep herder, the puli, originated in Hungary. At first glance it can be hard to tell which end is the front of the dog and which is the back! The puli's top coat is very thick and dense and forms what are called cords.

The Afghan hound is known for its long, silky coat.

Afghan Hound

English Springer Spaniel

Chinese Crested

The hairless Chinese crested looks a lot like the Mexican hairless except for hair on its head and tail and "socks" on its feet. Extra care must be taken with hairless dogs because of their sensitive skin. They need lotion to keep their skin moist as well as protection from the sun and cold.

The komondor is much larger than the puli, but it, too, has a top coat made of soft cords. Not only does its coat keep it warm outdoors, it also helps it blend in with the sheep to protect them better.

And then there are dogs with no hair at all! The Mexican hairless is one of the world's oldest breeds. Another name for this dog is the Xoloitzcuintle (pronounced show-low-its-queen-tlee). These dogs certainly don't know what it's like to have a bad hair day!

Some dogs have very unusual fur! The Rhodesian ridgeback is a large, powerful breed that was originally used in South Africa to hunt lions. These dogs have a line, or ridge of hair, on their back which grows in the opposite direction from the rest of their fur.

Old English Sheepdogs

Boning Up on Dog Care

Pets depend on their human companions for food, water, shelter, exercise, and love. So before getting a dog, it's important to remember that taking care of a dog is a big responsibility. But it's really not that hard, and it's fun!

Unlike people, dogs don't like surprises. Dogs like to eat, exercise, and rest at the same time each day. For a dog, the best practice is "the same old thing."

Poodle

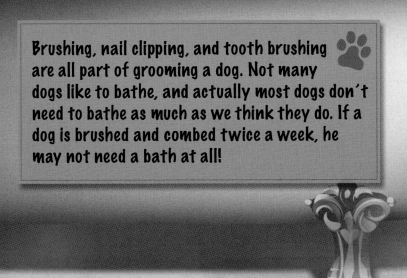

Brushing, nail clipping, and tooth brushing are all part of grooming a dog. Not many dogs like to bathe, and actually most dogs don't need to bathe as much as we think they do. If a dog is brushed and combed twice a week, he may not need a bath at all!

Golden Retriever

A little bit of training goes a long way. Teaching a dog to "sit," "stay," and "drop it" is pretty easy. Those three commands go a long way to keeping your dog safe and out of trouble. It's fun to teach your dog how to "shake" and "roll over," too!

The most important part of dog care is love. There's no schedule for that. Just give your dog lots of love, and he'll pay you back double!

Although it's easy to show a dog love with lots of treats, being overweight can lead to a lot of health problems for a pooch. It's good to check with a veterinarian to find out how much each dog should eat.

Dogs should be fed after they exercise. Eating before exercise can make a dog very, very sick. And did you know that chocolate can be poisonous to dogs? It's bad for their hearts. So, have a heart, and don't feel guilty about keeping that candy bar all for yourself.

17

Work and Play Like a Dog

Besides making great pets, some dogs have jobs to do! Guide dogs go to a special school to learn how to help people who are blind. A guide dog will go everywhere with its owner and make sure he or she walks safely.

Some dogs are trained to help people who are hearing impaired. They act as the person's ears, alerting them to doorbells, telephones, and lifesaving sounds, such as fire alarms and car horns. Small dogs make great "hearing" dogs. They don't need to be big and powerful; they just need to have good ears and a loud mouth!

Search and rescue dogs help police and firefighters find people who are trapped under buildings, lost in the woods, or buried under the snow.

German Shepherd Dog

Brave and smart, the German shepherd dog takes well to training and is widely used as a police and military dog. It was also the first breed to be trained as a guide dog for the blind.

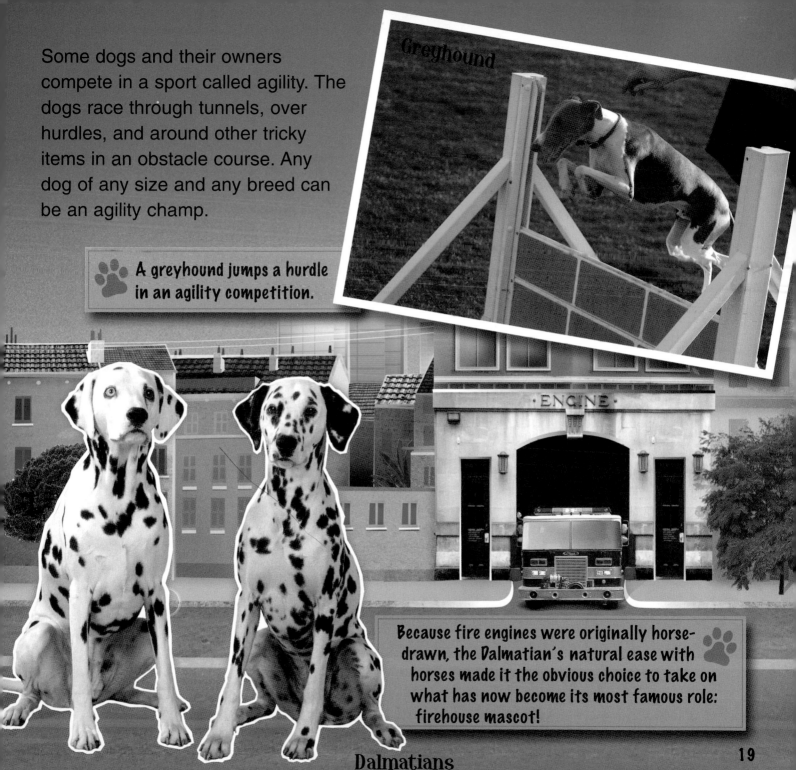

Some dogs and their owners compete in a sport called agility. The dogs race through tunnels, over hurdles, and around other tricky items in an obstacle course. Any dog of any size and any breed can be an agility champ.

Greyhound

🐾 A greyhound jumps a hurdle in an agility competition.

· ENGINE ·

🐾 Because fire engines were originally horse-drawn, the Dalmatian's natural ease with horses made it the obvious choice to take on what has now become its most famous role: firehouse mascot!

Dalmatians

19

From Around Here?

Dog breeds have come from all over the world and have been mixed and changed over and over again. The American water spaniel is one of only five dog breeds that actually originated in the United States.

Alaska

🐾 The Alaskan malamute was used by Inuits in Alaska to pull sleds. They date as far back as 3,000 years ago!

Alaskan Malamute

The Doberman pinscher originated in Germany. It was developed only a little over 100 years ago. A man named Louis Dobermann created this breed so he could have a good watchdog.

Though it, too, originated in Germany, people in France have loved the poodle for so many years that it is now often called the French poodle. Poodles were originally used to retrieve birds and ducks from the water and are well known for the fancy haircuts they are often given.

The Lhasa apso comes from the Far East. For about 2,000 years these little dogs were bred only by holy men and nobility in Tibet. Back then people thought that when the owner died, his soul went into the Lhasa apso's body.

What is a Schnoodle? Besides being fun to say, it is a designer breed of dog. First bred in the United States, it is a schnauzer mixed with a poodle and was created not to shed and to be "allergy-friendly."

🐾 China Is home to the char pei—which has a blue-black tongue!

Chinese Shar-Pei

China

Malta

Maltese

🐾 The Maltese is believed to have originated on the tiny island of Malta, near Italy. Women once carried these little dogs in their sleeves!

The Scoop on Groups

Because people have needed dogs for different things throughout history, dog breeds can be split into groups. The groups help you understand what the breeds within them were originally created to do:

1 Working Group

The big, hardy dogs in this group were originally bred to . . . work! Over the years they have been used to guard property and people, pull sleds, and even rescue people from the water. Includes: Alaskan malamute, Saint Bernard, rottweiler, Doberman pinscher, Great Dane, komondor, Newfoundland

2 Toy Group

Don't let their size fool you—these are small dogs with big personalities. They can be protective guard dogs as well as sweet lap dogs. Includes: Chihuahua, Maltese, Chinese crested, Mexican hairless, Pekingese

3 Terrier Group

Terriers are known to be feisty and stubborn. They were originally bred to chase and dig vermin (such as rats and foxes) out of their dens. The largest of the terriers is the Airedale. Includes: cairn terrier, Scottish terrier, Parson Russell terrier, fox terrier

4 Hound Group

Hounds were originally bred for hunting and tracking other animals. They are known for their keen sense of smell or sight, great stamina, and trademark baying sound. Includes: beagle, greyhound, Afghan hound, Rhodesian ridgeback, dachshund, bloodhound

5 Non-Sporting Group

Dog groups originally consisted of only sporting or non-sporting. All the other groups split off from these two categories. Whatever breeds remained were put in the non-sporting group, which is why these dogs vary so much in size, color, and fur. Includes: standard and miniature poodle, Dalmatian, Chinese shar-pei, Lhasa apso, bulldog

6 Herding Group

These working dogs became their own group in 1983. They excel at herding cattle and other animals. Their coats help them stay outside in very cold or hot weather. Includes: German shepherd dog, collie, Old English sheepdog, puli, Welsh corgi

7 Sporting Group

Dogs in this group were originally bred to be good swimmers. They are great at fetching and retrieving ducks and birds from the water as well as on land. Includes: Labrador retriever, golden retriever, English springer spaniel, cocker spaniel, pointer

There are, of course, mixed breeds that don't belong to any of these groups. And there are pure breeds that don't fit into any of these groups either. But there is one group that all dogs fit into . . .

Man's best friend!

Questions

1. Name three out of the seven main groups of dogs. (herding, working, hounds, sporting, non-sporting, terrier, toy)

2. What do you call a dog that is a combination of breeds? (mixed breed)

3. What did scientists find in caves in France? (paintings of people and dogs hunting together)

4. Scientists think that dogs originated _____ years ago. (60,000)

5. Scientists think that dogs are descendants of what animal? (the wolf)

6. Name an unlikely place in the United States where you can find coyotes. (Beverly Hills; Hollywood)

7. In 1997, scientists tested the _____ of wolves, jackals, and coyotes to see which were most closely related to dogs. (DNA)

8. What is a group of wolves called? (a pack)

9. The wild dogs in Australia are called _____. (dingoes)

10. What does the mother dog do to the puppy as soon as it is born? (licks it clean)

11. A puppy can't see or hear when it's first born. True or false? (true)

12. At what age can a puppy sit and stand by itself? (1 month)

13. A puppy is ready to leave its mother when it is about _____ weeks old. (8-10)

14. One reason that puppies like to chew so much is because they are _____. (teething)

15. Dogs have just one set of teeth throughout their lives. True or false? (false: they have baby teeth that fall out)

16. At what age is a puppy considered to be a grown-up dog? (18 months)

17. How old would you be in dog years if you were a two-year-old baby? (21 years old)

18. How old would you be in dog years if you were 8 years old? (45)

19. Puppies grow very slowly. True or false? (false: they grow quickly and are almost full size at just 1 year)

20. Dogs have 225 million cells that help them:
a. smell b. hear c. taste (a. smell)

21. Do dogs see well in the dark? (yes)

22. Which one of these breeds is a sight hound?
a. Maltese b. springer spaniel c. whippet (c. whippet)

23. What is a dog usually communicating when it rolls over? (you're the boss)

24. Name two things a wagging tail can mean. (the dog is happy, excited, or agitated)

25. What is one reason that dogs and wolves howl? (they miss their owners or pack members)

26. What are a dog's hackles? (hairs on the back of its neck and back)

27. What is unique about the basenji? (it doesn't bark)

28. Show what a dog does with its mouth to look ferocious. (pull your upper lip up to expose your teeth)

29. What is the tallest breed of dog? (Irish wolfhound)

30. What is Zorba, the Old English mastiff, known for? (it was the heaviest dog on record)

31. What is the smallest breed of dog? (Chihuahua)

32. Name a breed of dog that is longer than it is tall. (dachshund; basset hound)

33. What were dachshunds originally bred for? (to dig badgers out of their dens)

34. What was the Old English sheepdog bred for? (to herd sheep in cold weather)